365 ways to make the most of your marriage

JULIET JANVRIN AND LUCY SELLECK

Good Books

Intercourse, PA 17534
800/762-7171
www.goodbks.com

Acknowledgments

Page 3: quoted from The Alternative Service Book 1980, copyright © The English Language Liturgical Consultation (ELLC) and reproduced by permission of the publishers.

Original edition published in English under the title **365 Ways to Make the Most of Your Marriage** by Lion Publishing plc, Oxford, England. Copyright © 2001.

North American edition published by Good Books, 2002.
All rights reserved.

Text copyright © 2001 Juliet Janvrin and Lucy Selleck
Illustrations copyright © 2001 Stephanie Strickland
All rights reserved.
No part of this book may be reproduced in any manner, except for brief quotations in critical articles or reviews, without permission.

365 WAYS TO MAKE THE MOST OF YOUR MARRIAGE
Copyright © 2002 by Good Books, Intercourse, PA 17534
International Standard Book Number: 1-56148-349-4
Library of Congress Catalog Card Number: 2002022669

Printed and bound in Malta.

Library of Congress Cataloging-in-Publication Data
Janvrin, Juliet.
    365 ways to make the most of your marriage /
Juliet Janvrin and Lucy Selleck.
    p.cm.
    ISBN 1-56148-349-4
    1. Marriage--Quotations, maxims, etc. I. Title: Three hundred sixty five ways to make the most of your marriage. II. Selleck, Lucy. III. Title.
PN6084.M3 J36 2002
306.81--dc21   2002022669

To Bill   J.J.
To Stuart   L.S.

To have and to hold
from this day forward;
for better, for worse,
for richer, for poorer,
in sickness and in health,
to love and to cherish,
till death us do part.

Church Marriage Ceremony

Spring

1
Marriage, according to the law of the country, is the union of one man and one woman, voluntarily entered into for life to the exclusion of all others.

Civil Marriage Ceremony

2
The early days of marriage are full of surprises – some nice, some nasty!

3
Planning a wedding is like rolling a snowball down a hill: it gathers momentum.

4
The wedding day is important, but it is nevertheless only one day in what you hope will be a long and lasting relationship.

5

Spring is about new beginnings, green shoots of hope for the future. Your marriage has just begun.

6

Remember that you were married in the sight of God. Let God's gaze rest on and bless your marriage.

7
Marriage is a lifelong commitment. You stand before your nearest and dearest and declare your long-term intention to grow old beside another.

8
Masks don't work in marriage.
Be real, be vulnerable and without facade.

9
Marriage is like building a house.
Laying the foundations often means
digging tough ground.

10
Have independent friendships,
and share the interests and gains.

11
Don't always dump the dross of your day,
however broad the shoulders.

12
Realize that no one in this world
can fulfill all your needs and longings.

13
Contrary to popular belief,
love can mean having to say you're sorry!

14
Get home early from the office
and plan a treat together.

15
Keep your promises,
or don't make them.

16
Be a good timekeeper.
Don't keep each other waiting.

17
We all hold onto our secrets, but
within marriage they are *best* let go.

18
Notice how your partner looks,
and offer compliments.

19
Timing is of the essence
when saying something important.

20
Compromise may be necessary at Christmas.
All families celebrate differently.

30
Adjusting to married life can take time and involve a lot of tension!

31
Sometimes you must put aside some of the customs, ways, and thinking of the family you were raised in if you are to form a new one together.

32
Dirty socks are never appealing.
Don't leave yours lying around!

33
In a division of loyalties between your parents and your marriage partner, it is right to choose your partner. Your parents are the past; your partner is the future.

34
Don't let the sun go down on your anger.

35
High expectations may *be* hard to meet.

36
We all choose to spend our money in different ways, and this can cause divisions.

37
Whether you like it or not,
you marry into someone else's family.

38
Marriage is popular because it combines the maximum of temptation with the maximum of opportunity.

GEORGE BERNARD SHAW

39
Listening is the other half of talking.

40
Cupboards don't tidy nor freezers defrost without human intervention. Whose will it be?

41
Remember that your sexual needs and desires will not always match up. Be generous to one another.

42
Respect your spouse's hopes and dreams.

43
Respect the in-laws, even when it seems difficult. They raised the person you have chosen to spend the rest of your life with.

44
A child binds you together in new responsibilities and a shared future purpose.

45
New babies can threaten
the exclusivity of marriage.

46
It is wonderful to have someone
who shares our consuming interest
in our children.

47
Don't assume that your spouse's need for time on her or his own is a rejection. We all need space for ourselves.

48
Remember that your marriage is not your parents' marriage, and your partner is not your mother or father.

49
Cuddling can *be* enough to feel close.

50
Toddlers can invade your intimacy and are jealous for the attention you would like to give each other.

51
Find a babysitter you can trust, and get out and give each other time.

52
You may come from very different family backgrounds, even cultures. Time and understanding are needed to bring your diversities together.

53
Sharing the joy our children bring is a great unifying force.

54
Remember that everyone needs a
little unexpected spoiling
once in a while!

55
Take responsibility for your own feelings.
It is easy to blame your partner.

56
Exhaustion strains the relationship
of new parents.

57
Computers are a great advantage of modern life, but they can also take over. Know when to switch yours off!

58
Make it a priority to protect your marriage. Have your own private space away from the rest of the world.

59

Young children can test a marriage with their persistent physical demands. You both need a rest sometimes.

60

It is unreasonable to expect your partner to change if you are not prepared to make changes yourself.

61
Seduction should not be lost after the honeymoon.

62
Get in the habit early on of using "I feel" statements rather than "You are" statements.

63
Winning arguments does not always achieve a happy marriage.

64
Family and friends can be a great support, but don't ask them to take sides.

65
Goodbyes and hellos are always important. Seek out your partner with a loving word when you leave or arrive.

66
A shared faith enriches and sustains marriage.

67
It is a haven of security to see your partner across a crowded room of unknown party-goers.

68
Irrational jealousy corrodes trust. You may need to deal with the insecurities of the past that cause the possessiveness of the present.

69
Share your aspirations early on in
your marriage. You need to know each other's.

70
First babies call for a radical change
in matrimonial routine.

71
Housework builds up like layers of dust.
Don't leave it all to one person.

72
"Do it yourself" tasks done together
do not always enhance your relationship,
let alone your home.

73
Mobile phones are a great way to
communicate, but make sure it's your
partner you're speaking to!

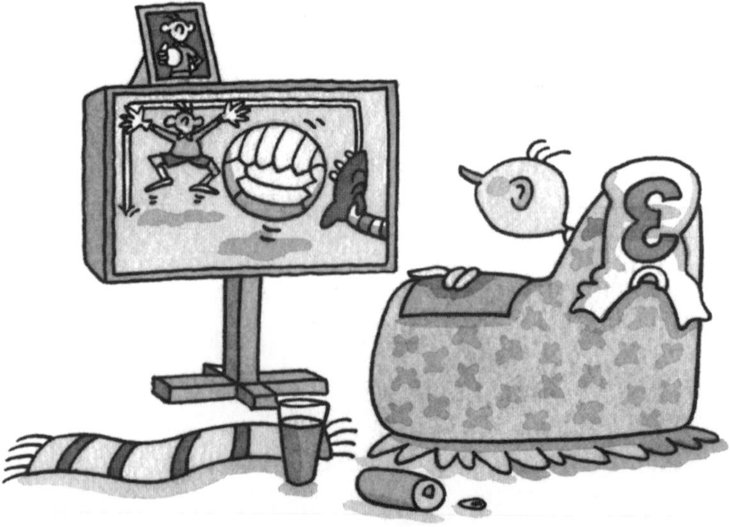

74
An excessive interest in sports
and a happy marriage rarely mix.

75
Decide which one of you is going to
be the bookkeeper and support your spouse
in it.

76
A quarrel can clear the air – or fill it
with things only meant at the moment,
but which are difficult to forget.

77
Tell your partner if a licked lip makes you loving but a stroked stomach makes you squirm!

78
Being married doesn't stop us from being attracted to other people, but it should stop us from doing anything about it.

79
Let the minor irritations of matrimonial life wash over you, or you will drown in a sea of annoyance.

80
Get to know each other's weaknesses and strengths with money, and discuss your hopes and fears.

81
A love note left on the pillow touches the heart.

82
Living with someone else and that person's habits is a matter of compromise.

83
Bullying spouses put down their partners in order to feel better about themselves.

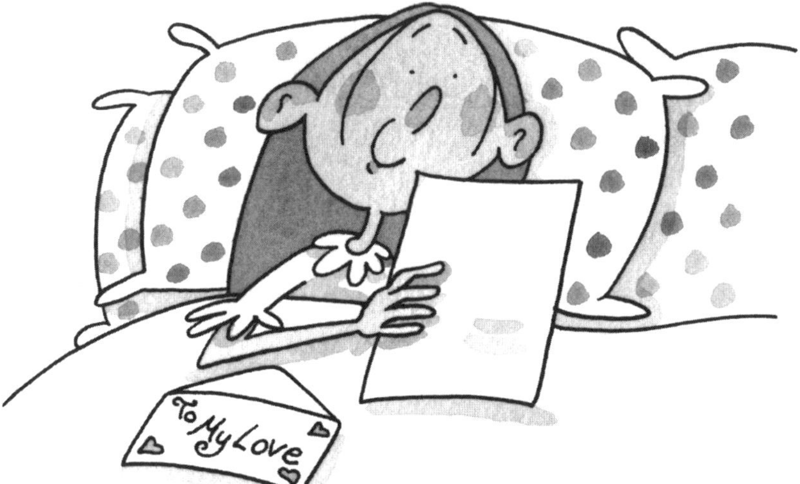
To My Love

84
Sometimes when you have come through a matrimonial bad patch, you can ask "What was that all about?" That is why it is worth staying until you are out the other side.

85
A lot of friction within marriage is a repeat performance of our parents' relationships. Watch out for the reruns!

86
Pleasing my partner should be more important than pleasing my parents. We are now adults in an adult relationship.

87
When your partner is saying something, listen. Don't just think of what you are going to say next.

88
Enjoy having different opinions.
We can't and shouldn't always
feel the same way.

89
When love flies out of the window
for a while, keep the window open
and marriage can survive.

90
Discuss the right way to squeeze the toothpaste before seeing your attorney!

91
For in what stupid age or nation
Was marriage ever out of fashion?

Samuel Butler

Summer

92

Summer is about long days of light and energy. Families grow fast. Sometimes the heat of the sun and life's cares can threaten a marriage with weariness and burnout.

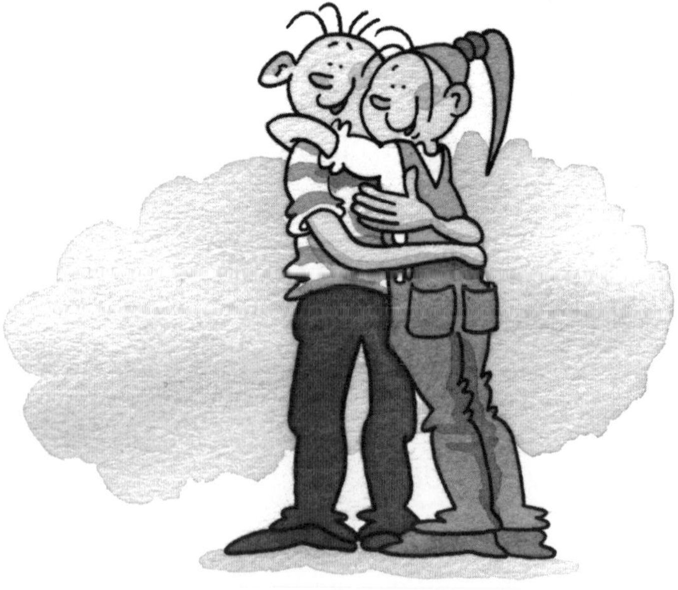

93
A quick hug is better than none.

94
Be brave enough to say what you want, although it may sometimes be hard.

95
It takes a little time to enjoy a holiday together. Give it just that.

96
Be a sun to your partner.
Light up his or her day with a loving gesture.

97
Constant complaining can become
extremely tiring in any relationship.

98
Forgiveness allows us to leave yesterday
behind so that we can enjoy today.

99
Christmas needs advance planning together in order to be a true time of celebration – for everyone!

100
Touching is the first step.

101
Don't assume what your spouse is thinking. Check it out.

102
"For richer, for poorer" is tough, when it's usually the latter.

103
Teenagers test any marriage, however strong.

104
Let roles and responsibilities be shared and flexible. Life does not always go according to plan.

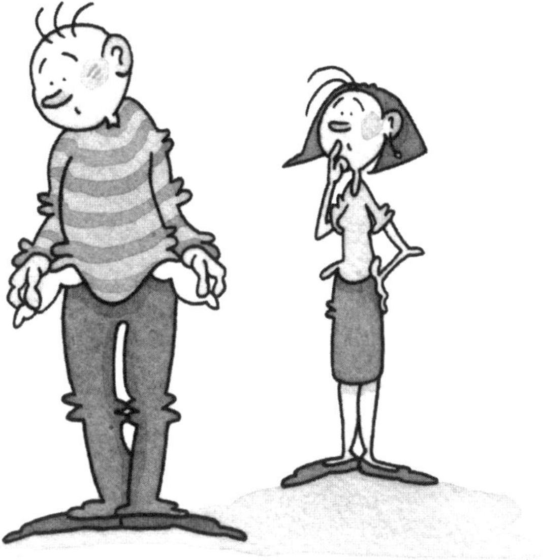

105
You married for *better*, for worse. If you always celebrate the first, then the *second* can usually take care of itself.

106
Don't deny that there's a problem if you know there is.

107
Be careful with each other's feelings. We are all more fragile than we seem.

108
Be generous in your attention to your partner. Don't slot your spouse into your life as an added extra.

109
Throwing things breaks more than plates.

110
Young people need the strength
of a united parental front.

111
If you have a past that is affecting
your marriage, then it is your responsibility
to deal with it, not your partner's. There
are people who can help.

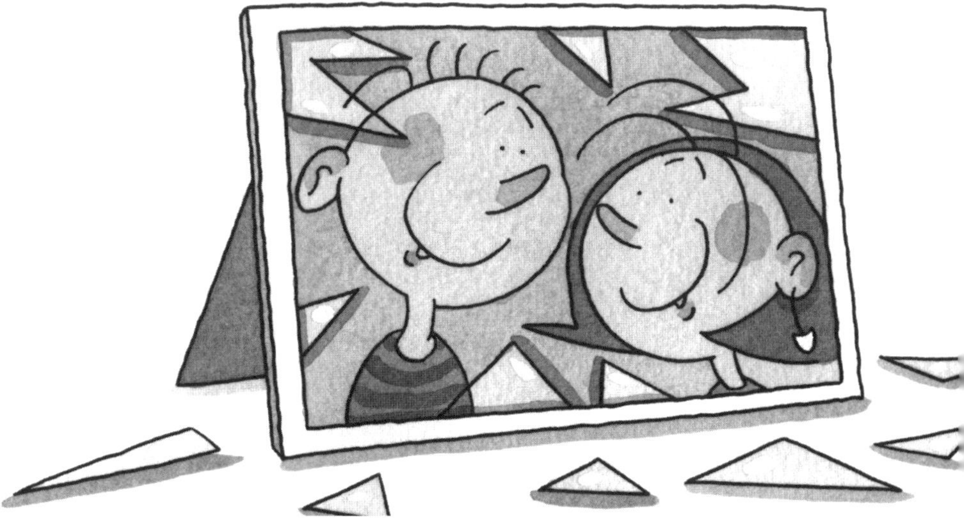

112
Discuss and plan the family finances together. Two heads are better than one.

113
God is the third strand that braids a marriage together to make a strong rope, able to withstand life's tensions.

114
Hurts shared are more likely to go away.

115
Don't assume there will be a tomorrow in your marriage if you take your spouse for granted today.

116
Adultery always begins with one small step,
one small incline along a rocky path.

117
Look after yourself.
Stress leaves little time for each other.

118
Spontaneous sex is wonderful,
but regular lovemaking sustains a marriage.

119
Beware of the friend who gives unsolicited criticism about your partner.

120
Move on. Don't harbor grudges and resentments.

121
Debt can overwhelm a marriage. Try to avoid it.

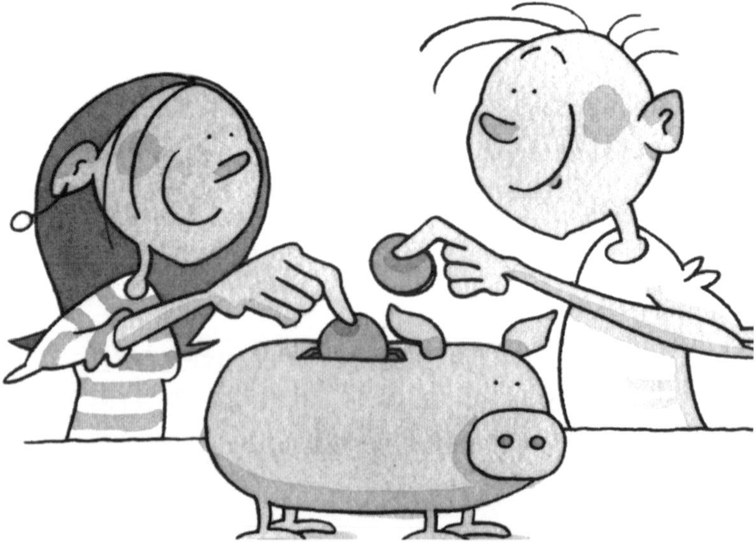

122
A marriage is like a bank balance. They both need regular investment.

123
Try to talk openly about a problem without blaming the other person.

124
Busy careers and lifestyles can be habit-forming. Break the habits once in a while.

125
Rainy days happen in everyone's life.
Put something aside for them.

126
Car journeys are not the best time
to corner your partner!

127
Be careful. Over-controlling your partner may lead to a break for freedom.

128
Any bereavement can rock a marriage, and the death of a child can devastate it. Seek help in your pain.

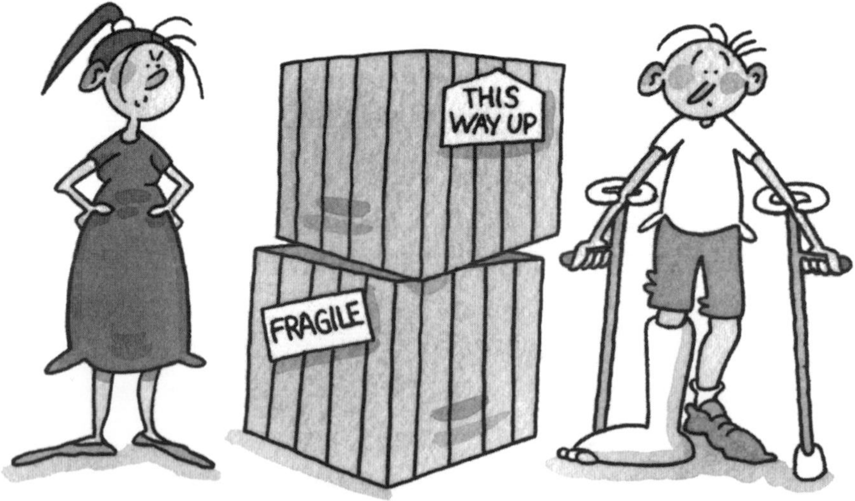
THIS WAY UP
FRAGILE

129
Moving to a new house is stressful at the best of times. Try not to do it at the worst.

130
Planning vacations can often *be* more fun than going on them!

131
Facing concerns about children together is a great comfort.

132
Give your partner the choice of doing a special activity she or he enjoys.

133
Where there is a joint will to save a marriage, then there is a way.

134
Back up your partner when disciplining children, even when you don't agree. Tackle the issues later.

135
Addictive behavior wrecks marriages and family life, but there is a cure and help for those who seek it.

136
Think about renewing your wedding vows every decade. God will bless that recommitment.

137
Change the venue. It's very refreshing.

138
Exercising together improves body, mood, and relationship.

139
Remember that a job is not always for life, but your marriage is.

140
Parents who love each other provide the *best* foundation for raising children.

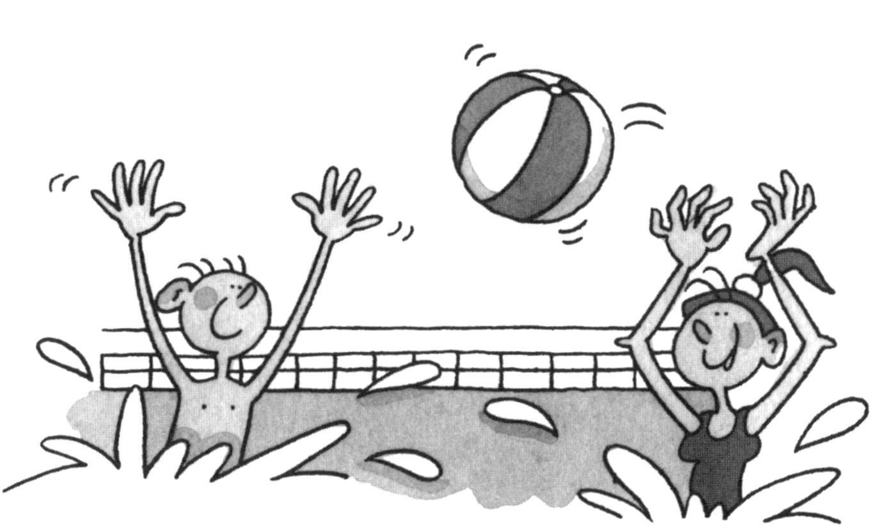

141
Support and encourage your partner in her career. Let your confidence in him travel with him into the workplace.

142
Wealth is not important, but money worries are.

143
A spouse who is not contributing properly to a marriage, whether physically, emotionally or financially, puts a strain on the partner.

144
If your marriage is in trouble, seek help sooner rather than later.

145
Recognize emotional and physical exhaustion in each other.

146
Infertility causes much pain and adjustment to the expectations of a marriage that yearned for children.

147
Quarrels can be like a runaway train. Know where the brakes are and use them!

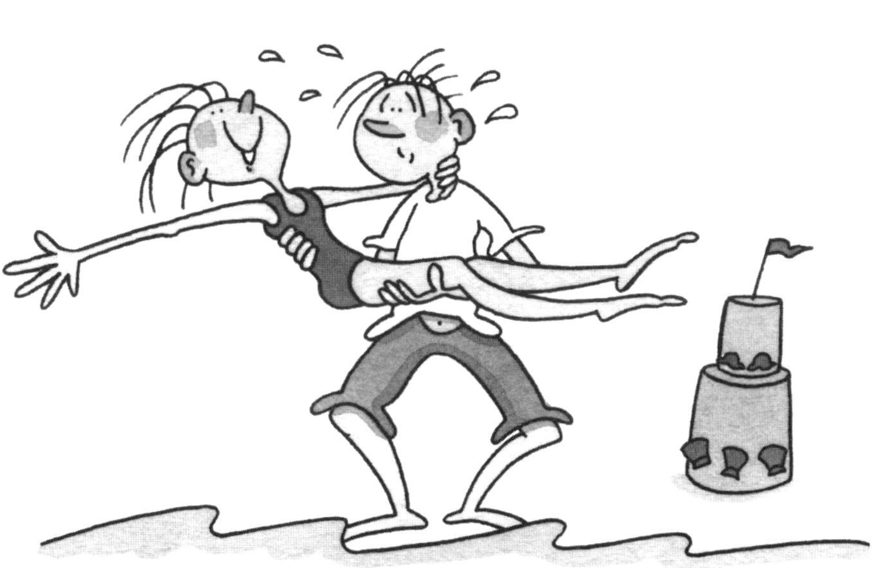

148
We need to be looked after
when we are feeling unwell.

149
You may have to face the fact
that your marriage does not meet your
expectations. But were your expectations
reasonable in the first place?

150
Yes, a romantic dinner for two does often end up with a passionate night in bed!

151
Share the everyday happenings with your partner every day.

152
The deceit of unfaithfulness is sometimes worse than the actions themselves.

153
Children don't have to hear your arguments to know that there is friction between you.

154
Remember that your marriage is a model for your children's future emotional relationships.

155
Teenagers remind you of your youth – and that neither of you are in it any longer!

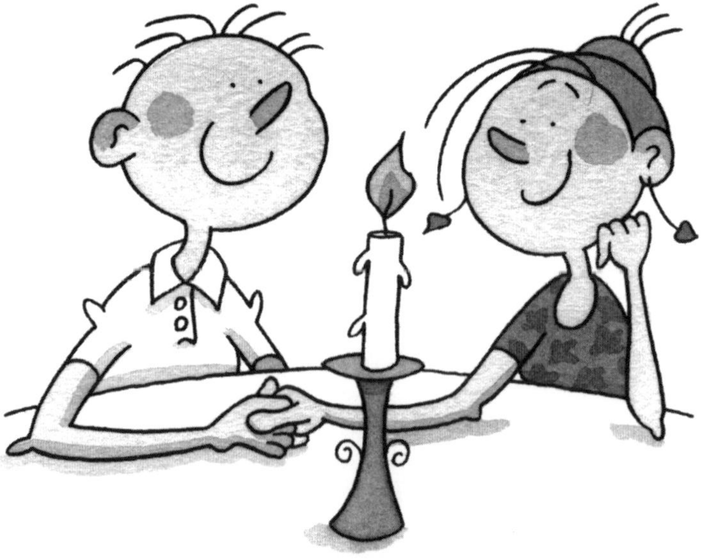

156
Candles are cheap to come by and create a *soft*, romantic mood.

157
Accusations, anger, and aggression do not change people, but love and understanding can.

158
Recognize that we all sometimes fail to provide what the other person needs.

159
Build a portfolio of shared memories to illuminate the dark days of your marriage.

160
When friends' marriages fail, it makes our own marriage vulnerable to attack.

161
Holidays can *be* as stressful as the rest of life, if not planned properly.

162
Listen and *be* attentive to your partner's concerns. Have you really heard what your spouse said?

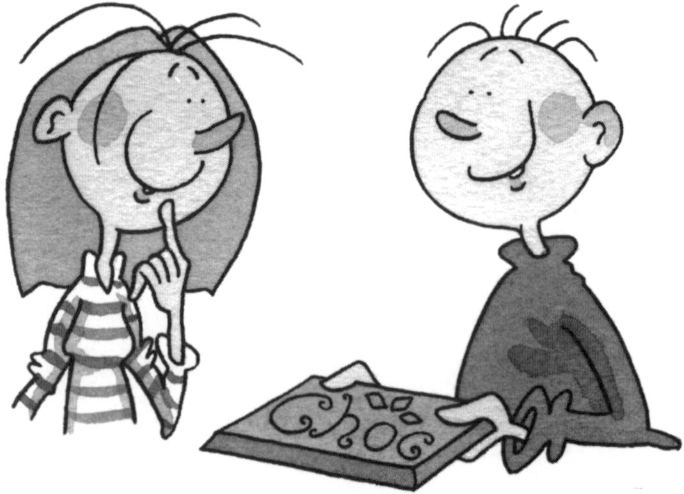
Choc

163
Showing you care can be as small as a favorite chocolate bar.

164
Wealth does not necessarily bring happiness to a marriage, but lack of it can bring unhappiness.

165
Tell each other if you don't understand – until you do!

166
Good friends enhance and strengthen your marriage. They do not seek to undermine it.

167
God is the cornerstone on which the house of marriage is built to withstand the storms of life.

168
Commit to saying at least one positive comment a day to your partner. We all need to hear good things about ourselves.

169
Trust can be quickly broken, but takes time to repair.

170
Shopping together only works
if you agree on what you like buying!

171
Create an oasis of matrimonial privacy
among the fragments of family life.

172
Getting along with each other's families
is a plus, but it is not always possible.

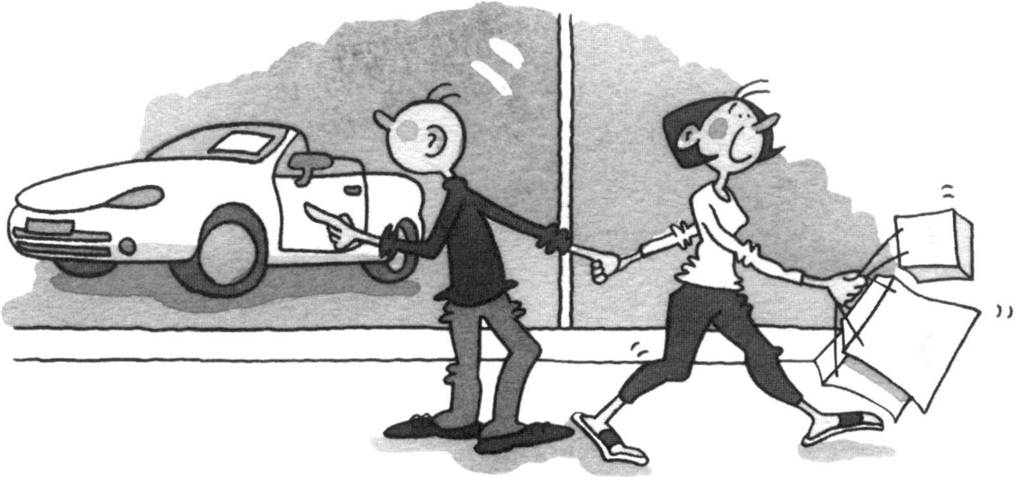

173
Adult behavior inspires an adult response.

174
It is easier to accept your partner for who she is than to try to change her.

175
Being kind to one another is
an act of will that becomes a habit.

176
A "normal" sex life for you as a
couple is the one you have, as long
as you are both happy with it.

177
Home is not always the best place to talk. Change the scenery.

178
Negative feelings can often be overcome by choosing to focus on the positive ones.

179
Sex can only improve if we tell our partners what improves it for us.

180
God, the best maker of all marriages, Combine your hearts in one.

WILLIAM SHAKESPEARE

Autumn

181

Autumn brings a slightly slower pace.
Children are growing up and leaving home.
This can be a new time of great color
and intensity in a couple's life together.

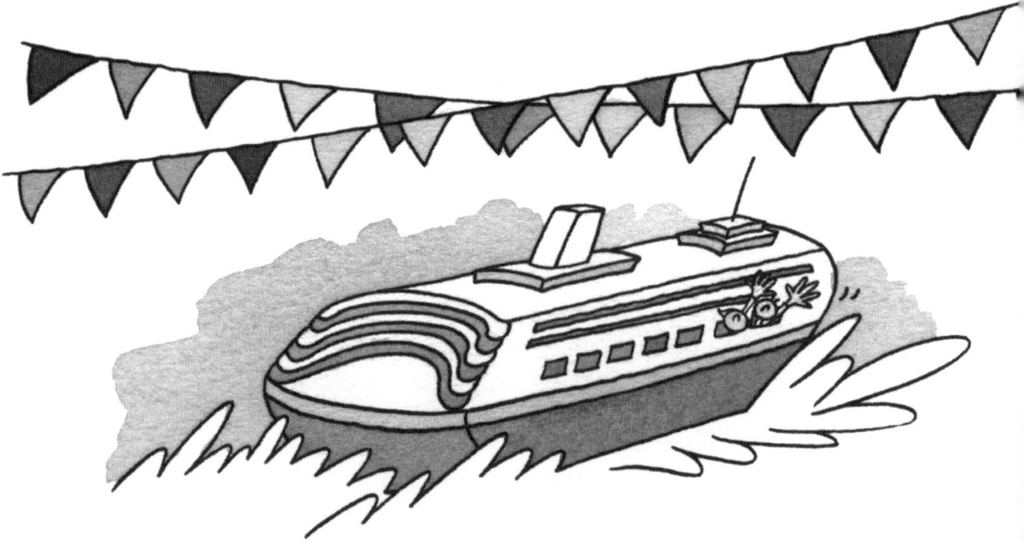

182
Children leaving home closes a chapter
in your lives, but also opens new horizons.

183
The joys of marriage are the heaven on earth,
Life's paradise, great princess, the soul's quiet,
Sinews of concord, earthly immortality,
Eternity of pleasures, no restoratives
Like to a constant woman.

JOHN FORD

184
Marriage is ideally a meeting of two minds, two bodies, and two souls in intimacy. Neglect any of these areas and problems may ensue.

185
Have another honeymoon. Go away for a night or two.

186
Old dreams may resurface or new dreams emerge for both of you. Be prepared to share them together.

187
Welcome different interests in each other's lives, but not to the detriment of your life together.

188
Looking at your marriage can be like looking at a painting. You need to stand back a little to get the whole view.

189
Buy a small present frequently, rather than a large one infrequently.

190
Change is like a torch that lights the footpath to a different way.

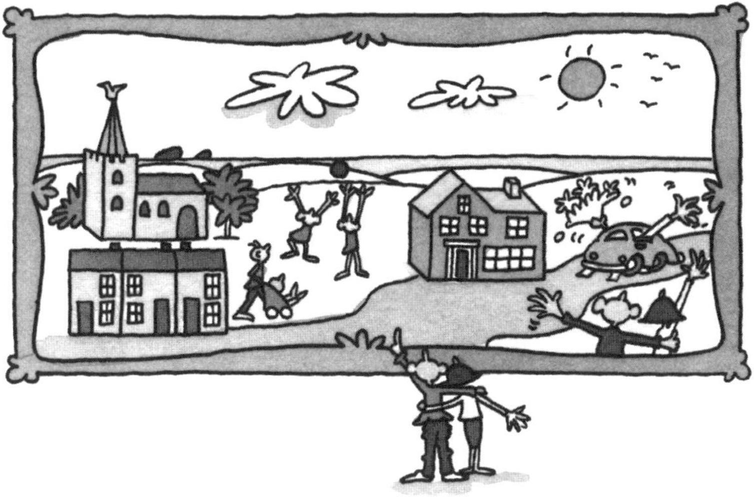

191
The empty nest syndrome can be balanced by plans to welcome freedom from parental responsibility.

192
Put yourself in your husband's or wife's shoes. They do not always feel as comfortable as your own.

193
Patience with one another when
you both want to be heard is difficult,
but there is time enough.

194
Needing some time alone is understandable.
Always wanting time alone is not.

195
Talking helps. Encourage one another.

196
Travel to destinations
you always wanted to go to.

197
Talk to each other on equal terms,
not as parent to child.

198
Share your sadness.
Your partner needs to know.

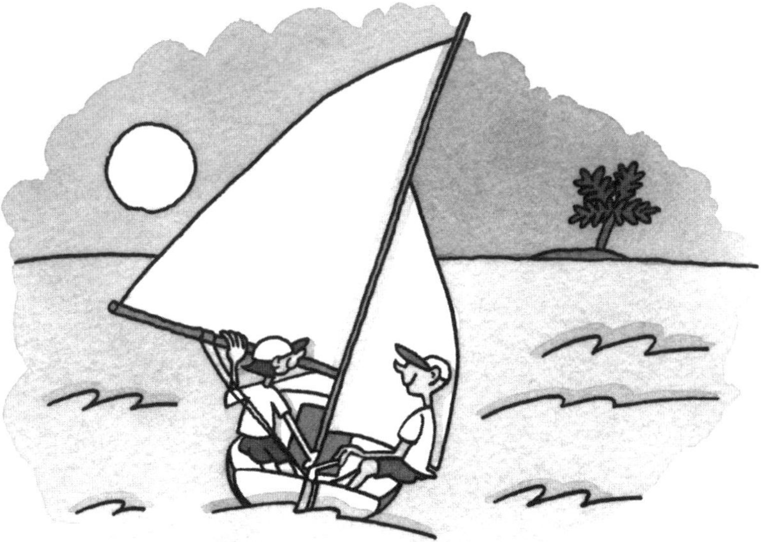

199
A wedding photograph sits on
the dressing table – a snapshot of
a promise. Commit to keeping it.

200
Light some candles,
and have a scented bath together.

201
Cook a favorite meal together, and take time to enjoy it.

202
Keep your bedtime for calm discussion. Don't turn it into a place of acrimony.

203
Remember the pastimes you both enjoyed, and revisit them.

204
Don't always be right. You're not, you know!

205
Admitting to one another that you are wrong is hard, but it comes with practice.

206
Soft words turn away angry feelings.
Hard words escalate conflict.

207
Don't swallow accumulated hurts.
They can grow into a well of rage.

208
Cuddles carry us through life's colder days.

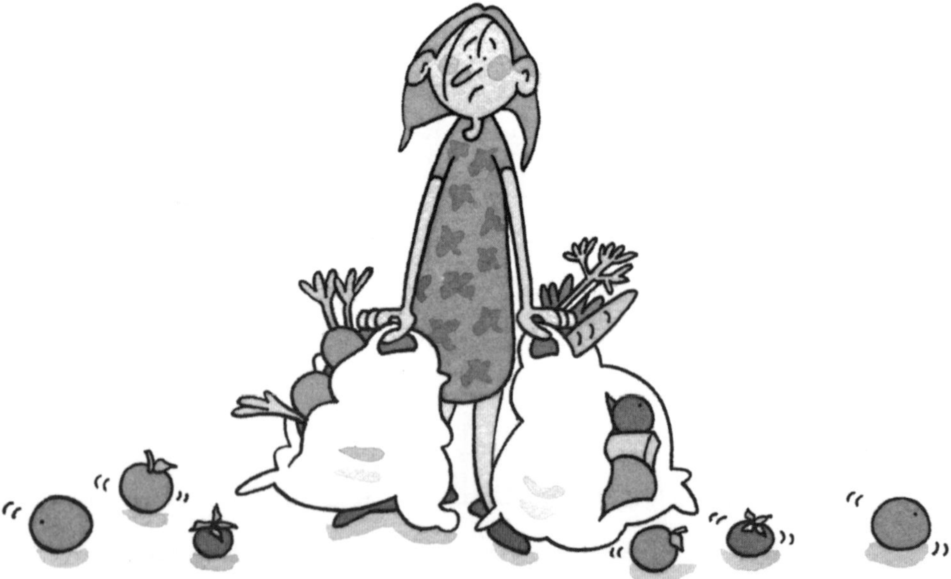

209
Ask for help.
Don't carry the burden alone.

210
An enduring sexual relationship is built on communication, acceptance, warmth, and friendship.

211
Adultery is usually a symptom and not the cause of marriage malaise.

212
Emotional turmoil can *be* shared,
however much of a muddle it all *seems*!

213
Each week plan for a "talk time" together.
Make it a priority.
Treat it as the most important non-negotiable
appointment that you have.

214
Plan to revisit favorite courting places.

215
Not enough outside company
can dull a marriage.

216
Sometimes we need to nurture
our partner like a good parent.

217
Like anything precious, marriage
should last a lifetime. Look after it!

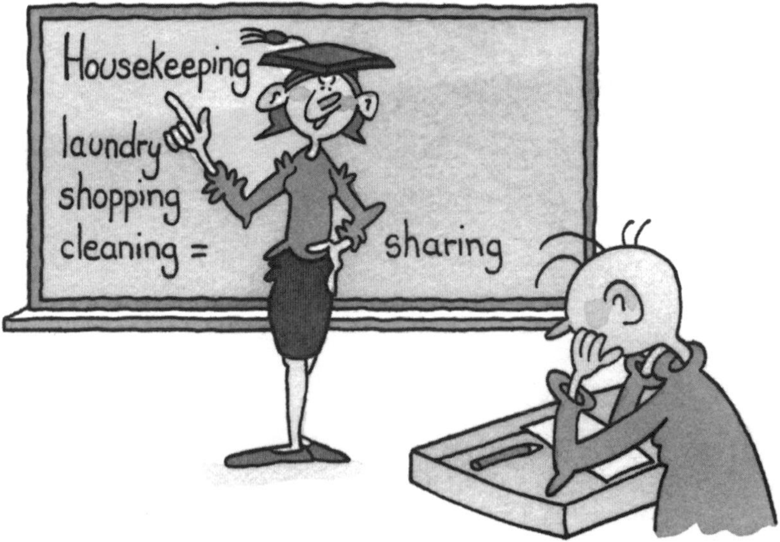
Housekeeping
laundry
shopping
cleaning = sharing

218
Giving your partner a good lecture does not make her or him a good student.

219
Don't leave skeletons locked in the cupboard. Otherwise, when you open it they will haunt you both.

220
Buy a treat for the partner who is caring for a sick relative.

221
Unexpected events may force you to reassess your life together.

222
Having separate friends and interests is important but should not replace your friendship together.

223
Give some thought to unrealized dreams. Some may be shared. Some can be realized individually.

224
Children prefer to leave happy, independent parents with a life of their own. Have you got one?

225
Love comes in waves through marriage.
Like surfing, you sometimes have to wait
on a calm sea.

226
Tuning into each other's needs can
be difficult if the transmission is faulty.

227
Explore new ways of getting closer physically.
Have you let things drift in recent years?

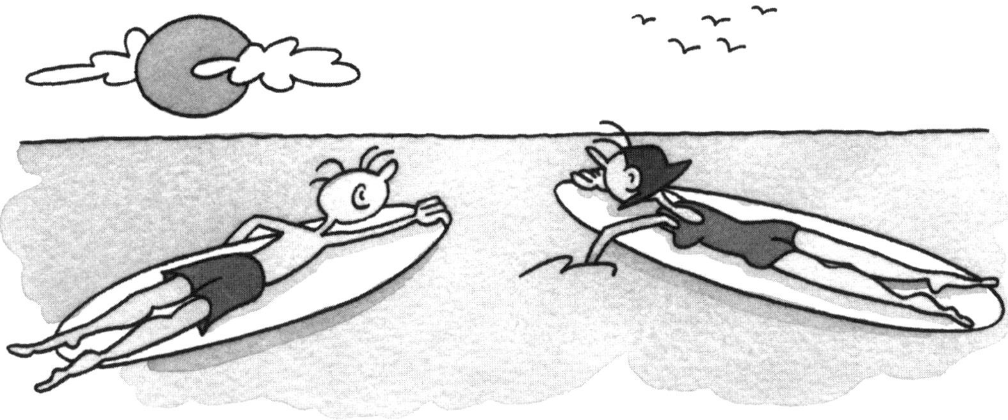

228
New roles demand new ground rules.

229
Fear of confrontation can stop us from sorting out difficult issues in our marriage, but lack of confrontation can lead to matrimonial breakdown.

230
Discuss change
and what it means to each of you.

231
Romantic love is not enough.
Marriage is built on action
as well as emotion.

232
Swap those household tasks you have always done. Give each other a break.

233
A critical spirit can create a stranglehold on a marriage.

234
Sharing a good laugh is a great medicine.

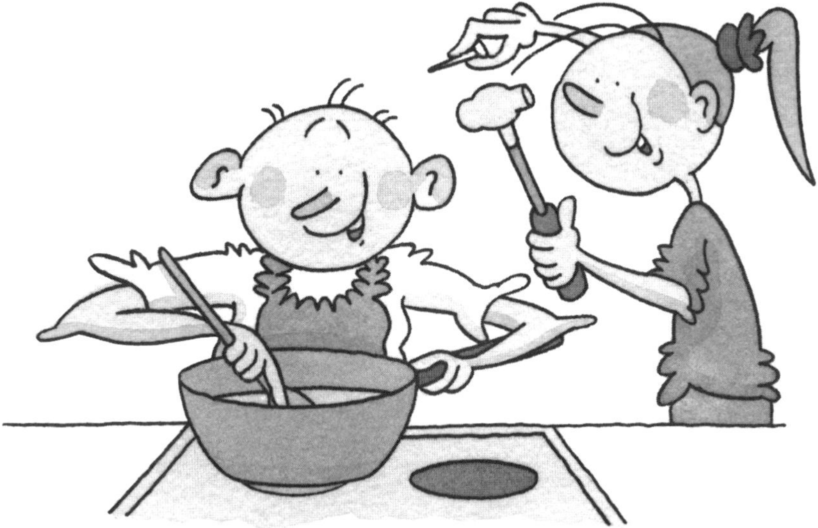

235
Forgive and forget past wrongs – again and again and again!

236
Contempt is a sore that opens the door to matrimonial destruction.

237
Remember that two are needed to engage in a dialogue.

238
Small, tender gestures touch us.

239
Listen to your partner with your eyes as well as your ears. Eyes are the doors to the heart.

240
Growth together only comes if you both embrace it.

241
It is often hard to articulate changes in ourselves to our partners when we have not yet made sense of them.

242
No one else can make us happy. We can choose to seek our own happiness at whatever age and stage of life.

243
A close physical relationship isn't just for the under-forties! This is a time for renewal.

244
Affairs have a message to give to a marriage; not necessarily that it is over, but that all is not well and that change is necessary.

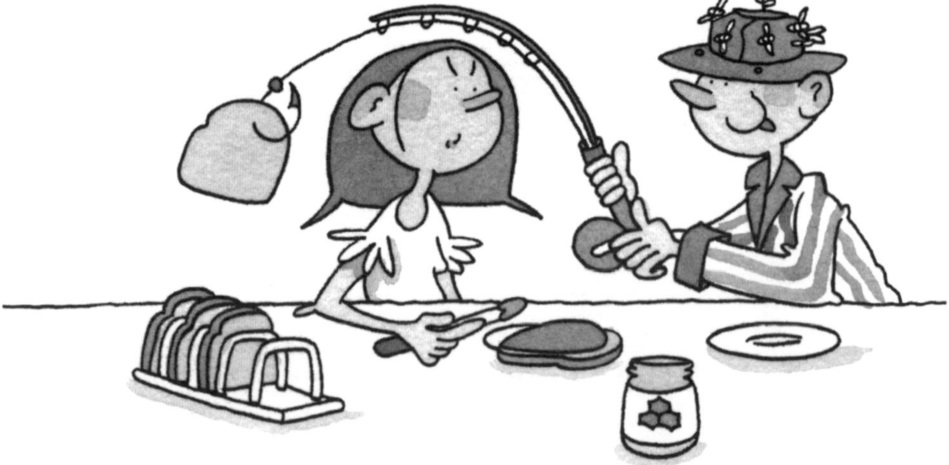

245
Hobbies are a great way of relaxing, but avoid having them take over your life and marriage.

246
Interrupting means that your partner cannot finish what he needs to say.

247
If you have something important to say, it is often how you say it, not what you say.

248
Look to each other to support,
not to blame.

249
Keeping sad feelings within
can create barriers between you.

250
Going out for a meal is
an opportunity to talk, not an
opportunity to sit in silence.

251
Take regular breaks,
even if they are short ones.

252
A job promotion probably means longer hours.
Review household chores.

253
Surprise your partner with
something unexpected. Predictability
can lead to boredom.

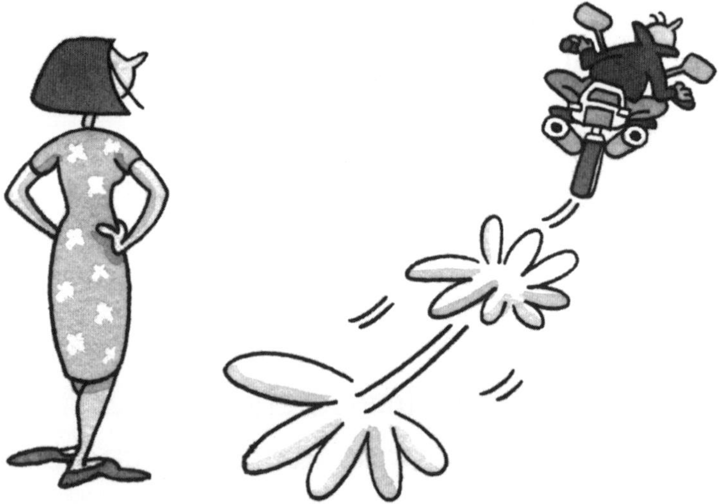

254
A midlife crisis is a time of turbulence. Be tolerant of your partner if she seems to be in one!

255
Be flexible in your outlook during this new phase.

256
Exchange ideas about changes you would like. Be prepared to accept each other's.

257
Tell each other if you don't understand.
Explain until the matter is clear to you both.

258
Pride in our grown children is
the enjoyment of a shared endeavor.

259
Love, acceptance, and tolerance
are keynotes of the matrimonial tune.

260
Marriage is about a partnership
and not a boardroom battle.

261
A long-lasting marriage is like being
wrapped in a security blanket. Hold it close.

262
Gossip after an evening out is one of the
pleasures of a married couple returning home.

263
Plant a plant that flowers at the same time as your wedding anniversary.

264
Pick up the phone and check on your partner's day. A loving voice is often a welcome respite.

265
Individual restlessness indicates that you need to make your marriage move on.

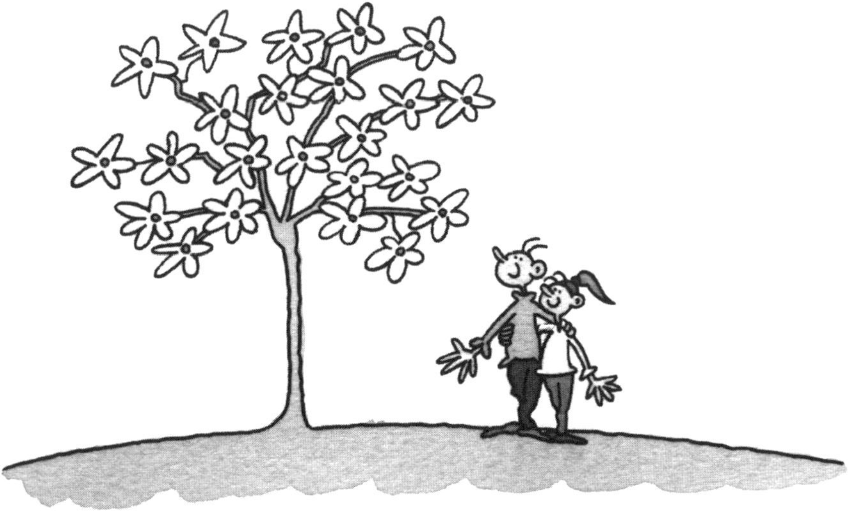

266
Remember your promise to "cherish" your partner. Wrap him in your warmth and affection.

267
Christmas can put an increasing strain on a couple's marriage. Change the routine and celebrate it differently this year.

268
A good relationship is about dependence in its most positive sense. Lean on one another from time to time.

269
Ill health and stress dampen the libido. You or your partner may have to wait patiently for restoration.

270
Don't soul-search and come to life-changing conclusions without mentioning the investigation to your partner!

271
A refining process can take place through the furnace of a good marriage that gradually eliminates the dross.

272
Help your partner look after her health.
You have an investment in her well-being.

273
The men that women marry
And why they marry them will always be
A marvel and mystery to the world.

HENRY WADSWORTH LONGFELLOW

Winter

274

Winter is about drawing the curtains and staying warm inside. Your years of commitment to one another are like a well-made fire that glows against the chill of old age.

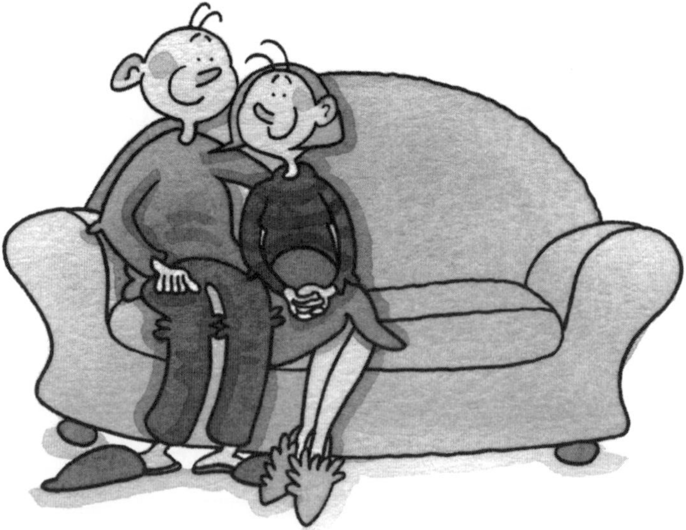

275
Sitting in your favorite armchair every night is cozy, but share the sofa instead.

276
All love at first, like generous wine,
Ferments and frets until 'tis fine;
But when 'tis settled on the lee,
And from th' impurer matter free,
Becomes the richer still the older,
And proves the pleasanter the colder.

Samuel Butler

277
Bodies change, wrinkle, and wither, but the beloved's eyes remain constant — a window to the person you fell in love with long ago.

278
Keep alive memories of courtship in special places, songs, and letters.

279
We find growing old hard sometimes. Be sensitive to the changes in each other.

280
Don't allow hours of differences
to drift into days, months, and years.
Address them – life is short!

281
New paths make way for new directions.
Try taking them together.

282
"In sickness and in health" – the former often
becomes a painful reality in our winter years.

283
Grandchildren recapture the spring days of our children's youth – days that we can remember together.

284
Aches and pains become an interesting topic of conversation for the more mature couple!

285
A present without a reason is a good reason to give one.

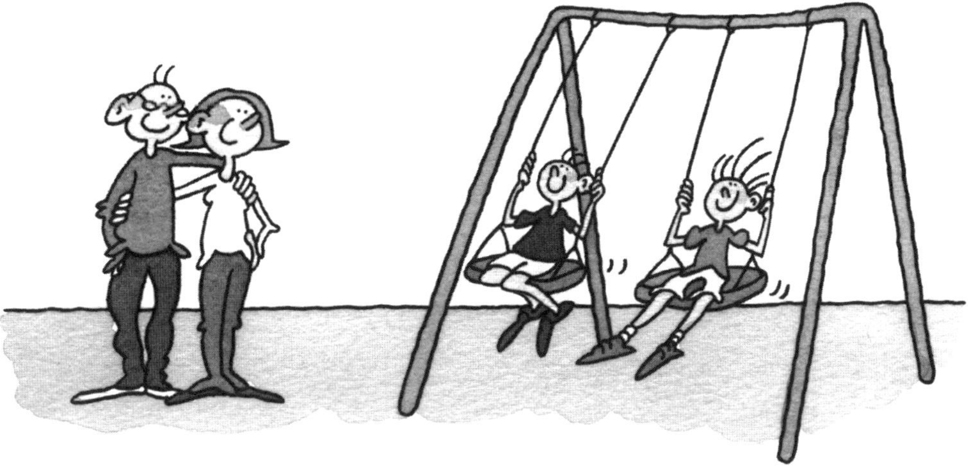

286
As it matures, companionship becomes one of the most important and valued components of married life.

287
When our partners are in pain, we feel helpless.

288
We all suffer from periods of emotional vulnerability and need extra sensitivity and care.

289
Marriage is like a lifelong investment. Dividends grow and mature and are paid out in the later years.

290
A mature and loving marriage is like the sweetness of a much loved melody.

291
A mature but embittered marriage is a twisted cacophony of sound.

292
Gardening together opens up the doors
of your marriage.
Plan who does different tasks,
so that you don't tread on each other's boots!

293
Change is difficult, but it can
also be the road to pastures new.

294
Remember the words "I love you."

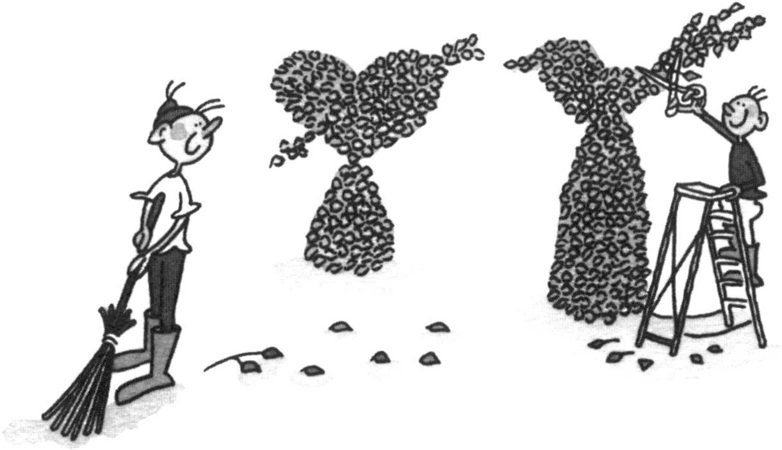

295
Tolerance of each other's faults results in a gentle and heartwarming acceptance that allows give-and-take.

296
Tell your spouse how much he has meant to you, before it is too late.

297
Sharing grandchildren is one of the great blessings of a long-lived marriage.

298
Nursing a failing partner is very hard.

299
The more you have had to work at a marriage, the more you can appreciate its long-term endurance.

300
Reassure yourself in times of doubt, when your partner is gravely ill, that you can only do your best.

301
The aging body causes insecurity. We all need reassurance to deal with a changing shape and a skin that seems too big!

302
Retirement brings with it mixed blessings. Count those blessings, but be flexible with the changes.

303
Just holding hands creates warmth.

304
Wisdom in later life is a very useful resource. Tap into it in your marriage.

305
They say old habits never die, but some need to do just that. Breaking the habits of a lifetime allows new ideas to develop.

306
We never stop learning new things about our partners.

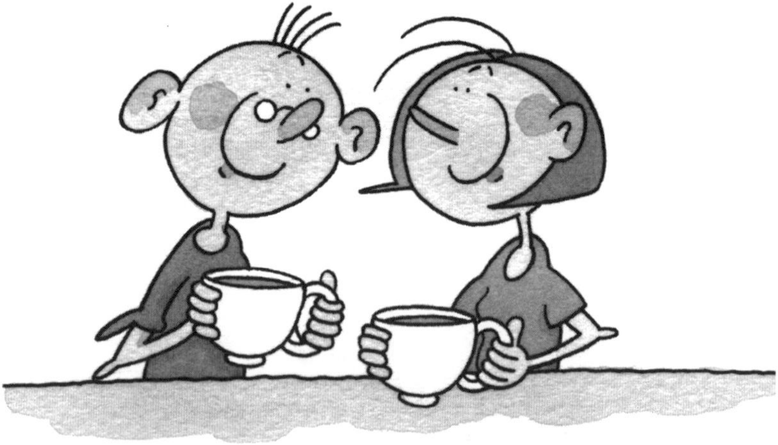

307
A cup of tea together is a comfort at any time of day.

308
Part of the art of negotiation is the willingness to compromise.

309
Remember that the caregiver, as well as the patient, needs attention when one of you is sick.

310
Interest and involvement in the younger generation keep us in the flow of life.

311
A glass of wine, take-out food, and an old film you saw together in the cinema long ago equals happy relaxation.

312
Old friends buoy up old marriages like a welcome float.

313
Hearing the same stories retold gets easier as you become more forgetful yourself!

314
We may need to be the eyes or ears of our partners in old age.

315
Marriages and people change over the years together. What you did understand about each other, you may not now.

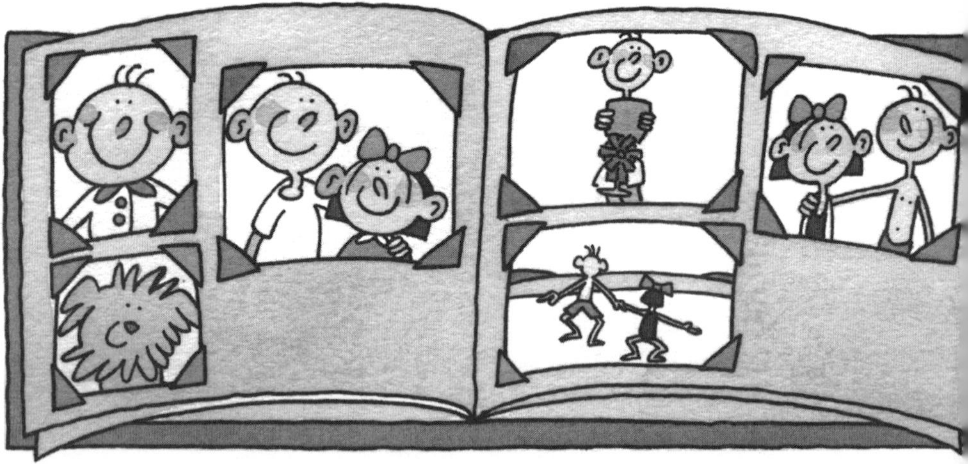

316
Look back in the photograph album at happy days. It can *be* lovely to reminisce.

317
The time and experience you have together in your later years give you the tools for when things get tough.

318
Give your partner something that represents the *best* in your marriage.

319
Silence is golden.
Enjoy the peace and quiet between you.

320
Going to bed at different times
can become a lifelong habit. Break it
once in a while and have a cuddle.

321
Routine is a good anchor but can become
monotonous. Change it and enjoy the fresh air.

322
Stay in bed together one day, open a box of your favorite chocolates, and relax. You're allowed to be indulgent in your old age!

323
The marriages of our children are full of their own emotions. Stay clear of interfering and trying to resolve things for them.

324
Age and time need not destroy love.

325
A walk together can be
a wonderful shared pleasure.

326
Having and holding are the
alpha and omega of marriage.

327
As the years go by, it is easy
to lose sight of the first time
you set eyes upon each other.

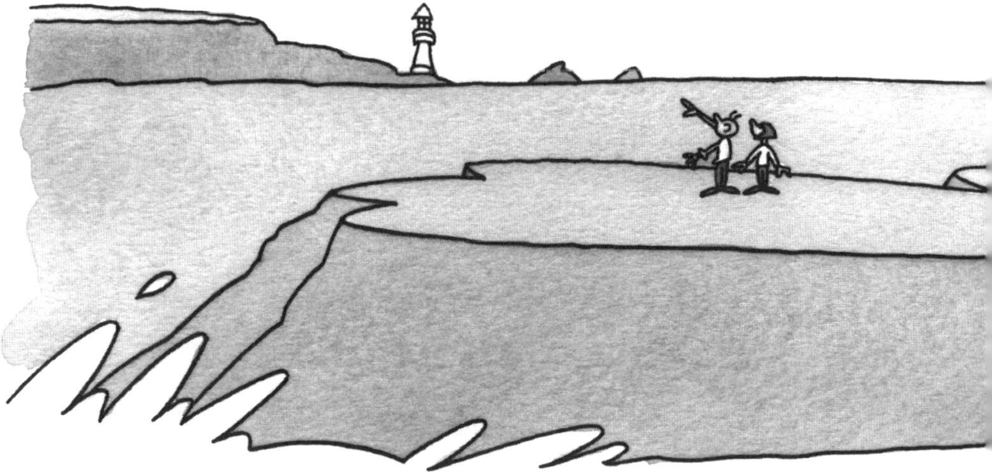

328
The changes of old age may
change the balance of your marriage.

329
Have a laugh together. Humor
is the bedrock of a long marriage.

330
Celebrate your wedding anniversary.
Your marriage is an achievement!

331
Creating change in your relationship can add new depth and color.

332
Just hearing your partner's problems is helpful. There is not always a solution.

333
A person who is grieving needs to talk it through. Give your partner time.

334
Words written in a love letter resonate through the years in a way that spoken words cannot.

335
When we are older, we are often too proud to seek help. It is then that we need to be sure that we have nothing further to learn.

336
Put things to look forward to in your calendar, and anticipate them together.

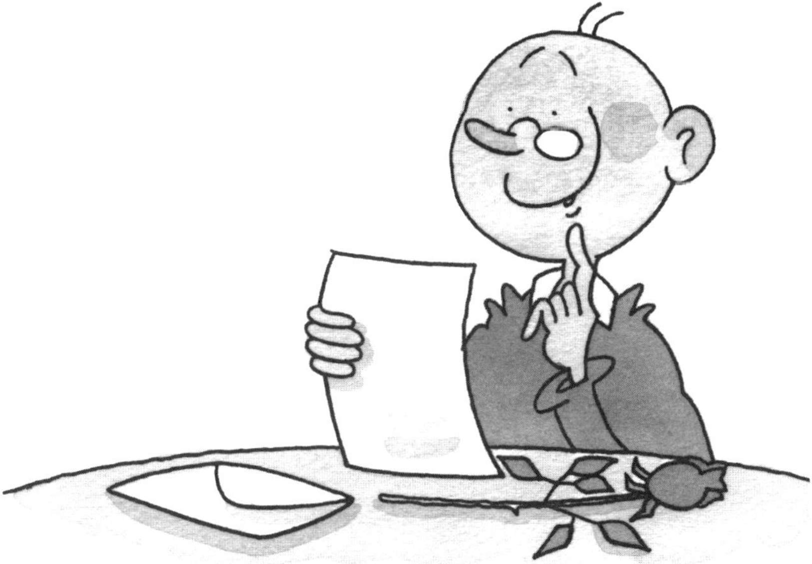

337
None of us wants to be patronized by our nearest and dearest, even if we have been together for half a lifetime!

338
It is peculiar how the irritating traits of yesteryear can become endearingly familiar after long years of acquaintance.

339
Inside a frailer body is the same lover.

340
Your grandchildren and great-grandchildren are a reminder of how your marriage will continue to be a part of future generations.

341
The difficulties of old age can be irritating to a partner who is not suffering from those particular ones!

342
When old friends die, it is a bitter blow.

343
Having arms wrapped around you
is often more important than sex.

344
Discuss what dying means to you,
and help your partner to prepare.

345
A good marriage is like a harbor that
you have returned to again and again
after a life of journeys on the open sea.

346

If our partners lose their minds, it is as if they have left us to go to another land. The pain can be immense.

347

Music has many moods. So does lovemaking.

348

Find out what turns your partner on – and turn it on. Sometimes what we enjoy changes as we get older!

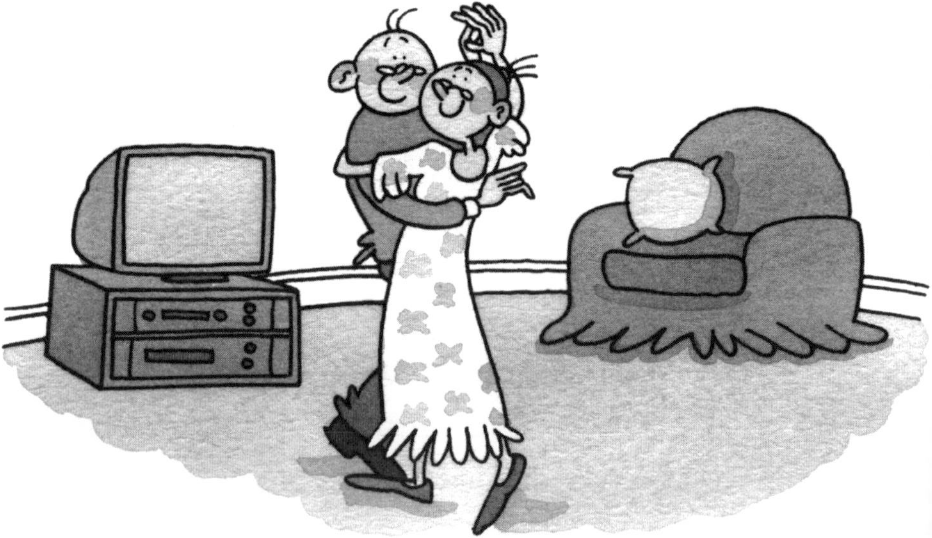

349
Switch the TV off
and put on your favorite old music.

350
Good sex is not the prerogative of the young,
although they would like us to think so!

351
Marriage is not like an automatic car.
You have to change gears to get somewhere,
even in the later years.

352
It is a great relaxation to be with a person who has seen you grow and mature throughout a lifetime – and loved you through it!

353
The last and one of the most loving things you may *be able* to do for your spouse is to sit and hold her hand.

354
In a happy marriage it is the wife who provides the climate, the husband the landscape.

Gerald Brenan

355
It is good to see other couples, old friends, who have endured as we have.

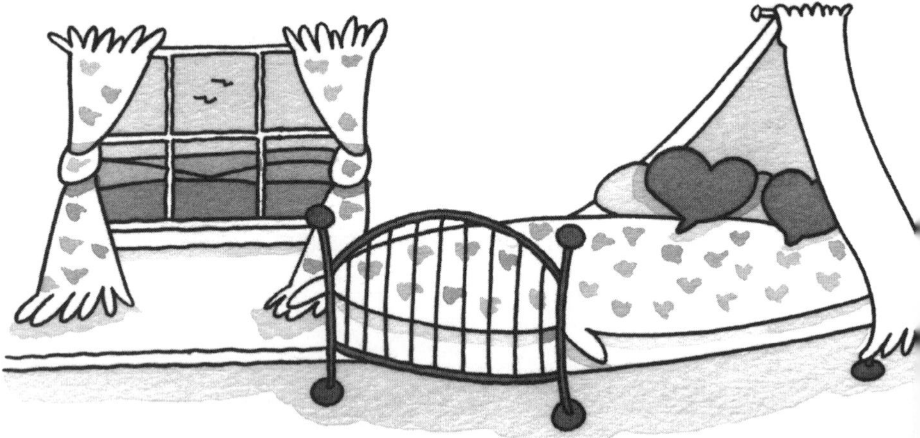

356
Redecorate your bedroom to be as you have always wanted it. Make it a special haven for you both.

357
A lifelong partner is like a watchmaker who knows just how the cogwheels turn within your head.

358
Count your blessings together.

359
Fear of loss can color the late days of marriage. Enjoy and savor your time together.

360
Each day reflect on a happy day that you remember from the past.

361
The devotion of one for another is grace from God combined with human endeavor.

362
A long marriage is a blessing, not just to those who have lived it, but to their children and their children's children.

363
When all else fades away, a long marriage is a testimony to the endurance of a loving human relationship that reflects the eternity of the soul.

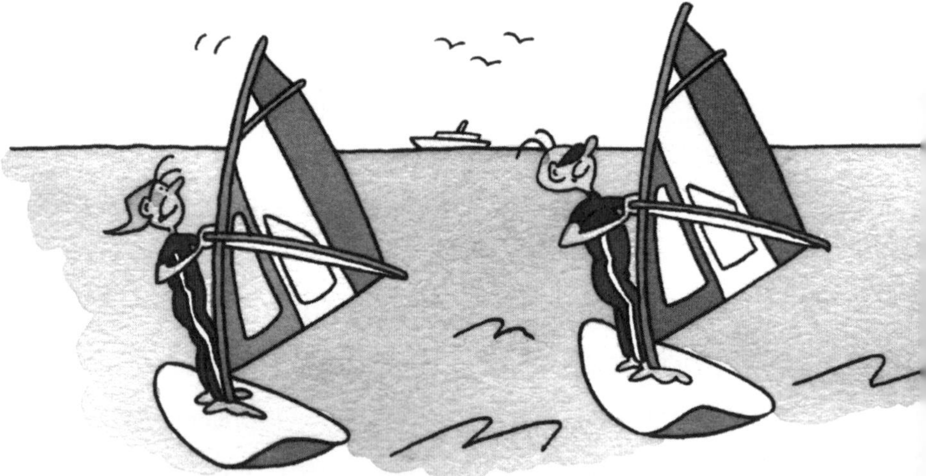

364
While there is life and energy,
be as energetic as you both can be.

365
To every marriage there are *seasons* – spring, summer, autumn, and winter. To each and every season life will bring its own joy, happiness, sadness, and difficulties. If a husband and wife face these united, with faces turned towards one another, then God will surely bless their embrace.